Retro Recipes

2021

The Most Popular Vintage Recipes from the 1960

CONTENTS

INTRODUCTION

Have you ever been struck by food nostalgia? Well, that happens to most of us all the time whenever we miss our grandma's cookies or delicious pies our moms used to make. Each decade and era come with its own set of popular meal. For instance, fast food was never that popular in the first of the 20th century; it was by the end of it.

Some meal evolves, recipes changes or new dishes emerge with time. There are lots of vintage dishes that are centuries old, and mankind still likes to have them, like the classic beef and lamb stews, the soups and fire-roasted chicken, all because we cannot get enough of them.

Similarly, there are other traditional dishes that we all seem to be forgetting about, but they are must-try food for every vintage food lover. In this cookbook, you will get to find all the classic 1960s vintage recipes in one place. Now you won't have to look for those recipes in old rusty closets or cabinets, as you can have them in her, categorized into different sections.

Why from the 1960s? You must be asking yourself this question right now! Well, when it comes to food, the 1960s is marked as the era of the culinary revolution in America. That's right! It was the period when people like Alice Waters and Chez Panisse start to set up a movement in motion for the New American Cuisine, and international cooking practices or exotic and healthy ingredients were brought into use. Before this period, there various regional cuisines and but the 1960s brought a nationwide New American cuisine with itself. As time passed, in few years, this cuisine became widely popular. During this period, the use of new kitchen technology was also on the rise, which greatly stretched the basic American menu and gave people a wide range of options to cook. Thus, the era is perfect for picking your favorite vintage recipes to try.

So, there were all sorts of rising influences over the culinary culture and traditions of the country during that period. Eating practices were not only changing, but the food itself had become part of the activism during those years. That's what makes the 1960s food important for all. Here are some unforgettable delights from this era. Give these meals a try and see how they take you back in the retro years.

ENTRÉE RECIPES

Roasted Chicken

This is a family-favorite roasted chicken that's perfect for any dinner feast. My Aunt Eunice's French-inspired version of the recipe has been loved by everyone in the family for years.

Serves 4 | Prep time 15 minutes | Cooking time 1 hour 20 minutes

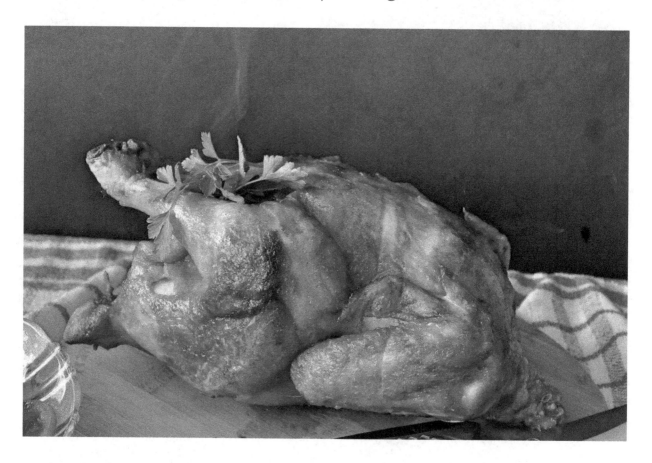

Ingredients
Non-stick cooking spray
1 (3½-4-pound) whole chicken, neck, and giblets removed
Salt and ground black pepper, as required
1 lemon, sliced thinly
1 small onion, quartered
4-6 celery leaves
¼ cup butter, softened

Directions

1. Preheat your oven to 425°F (218°C).
2. Grease a wire rack with cooking spray and arrange it in a roasting pan.
3. Season the cavity and outside of the chicken with salt and black pepper evenly.
4. Stuff the cavity of the chicken with lemon, onion, and celery leaves.
5. Rub the chicken with butter evenly.
6. With kitchen twine, tie the drumstick ends together.
7. Arrange the chicken into the prepared roasting pan, breast side up.
8. Roast for about 15 minutes.
9. Now, reduce the temperature of the oven to 350°F (177°C).
10. Baste the chicken with pan juices and roast for about 60-65 minutes, basting with pan juices after every 8-10 minutes.

Chicken Divan

Created in New York City at Chatham Hotel by Chef Lagasi in the late 50s, this is one of the most classic American casserole dishes that became very popular in the 1960s. This was one of the first recipes my grandmother taught me and to this day, I treasure this recipe that she passed down to her children.

Serves 6 | Prep time 15 minutes | Cooking time 30 minutes

Ingredients
Non-stick cooking spray
2 (10½-ounce) cans condensed cream of chicken soup, undiluted
½ cup mayonnaise
¼ cup white wine
1 teaspoon fresh lemon juice
½ cup breadcrumbs
1 tablespoon butter, melted
4 cups cooked chicken, chopped

24 ounces frozen broccoli florets, thawed
½ cup shredded cheddar cheese

Directions

1. Preheat your oven to 350°F (177°C).
2. Grease a 9x13-inch baking dish with cooking spray.
3. In a bowl, add cream of chicken soup, mayonnaise, wine, and lemon juice and mix until well combined.
4. In another small bowl, add breadcrumbs and butter and mix well.
5. In the bottom of the prepared dish, place the chicken and broccoli and top with soup mixture, followed by the butter mixture.
6. Bake, uncovered for about 25-30 minutes.
7. Serve hot.

Chicken à la King

This recipe rose into popularity in the 1960s. It's one of the favorites of my grandfather, which is why my grandmother always cooked it for him.

Serves 6 | Prep time 15 minutes | Cooking time 8½ hours

Ingredients
1 (10¾-ounces) can low-fat condensed cream of chicken soup, undiluted
3 tablespoons all-purpose flour
¼ teaspoon ground black pepper
Pinch of cayenne pepper
1 pound boneless skinless chicken breasts, cubed
½ cup red bell pepper, seeded and chopped
1 celery rib, chopped
¼ cup onion, chopped
1 (10 ounces) package frozen peas, thawed
2 tablespoons diced pimientos, drained

Directions

1. In a 3-quart slow cooker, add soup, flour, black pepper, and cayenne pepper and mix until smooth.
2. Add the chicken, bell pepper, celery, and onion and stir to combine.
3. Set the slow cooker on "Low" and cook, covered for about 7-8 hours.
4. Uncover and stir in peas and pimientos.
5. Set the slow cooker on "Low" and cook, covered for about 30 minutes.
6. Serve hot.

Chicken Kiev

Chicken Kiev is an old Russian dish from St. Petersburg. It became popular in America in the 1960s through Russian restaurants. This is my great-grandmother's recipe.

Serves 4 | Prep time 25 minutes | Cooking time 19 minutes

Ingredients
2 garlic cloves, minced
Salt, to taste
2 tablespoons fresh flat-leaf parsley, chopped
6 tablespoons unsalted butter
4 (8-ounce) skinless, boneless chicken breast halves, pounded to ¼-inch thickness
Ground black pepper, to taste
1 cup all-purpose flour
2 eggs, beaten

2 cups panko breadcrumbs
2 cups vegetable oil
Pinch of cayenne pepper

Directions

1. In a mortar and pestle, grind garlic and a pinch of salt until garlic is completely smashed.
2. Add parsley and mix until completely combined.
3. Add butter and with mortar and pestle, mix until well combined.
4. With a plastic wrap, wrap the butter and refrigerate for at least 15 minutes.
5. Season the chicken breasts with salt and black pepper.
6. Place ¼ of the butter mixture in the center of each chicken breast.
7. Fold the narrower end of each chicken breast up over the butter to form a tight pocket.
8. Gather the sides of each chicken breast to the center to shape into a ball.
9. Using plastic wrap, cover each chicken breast ball tightly and arrange it onto a large plate.
10. Freeze for about 30 minutes.
11. In a shallow bowl, mix the flour and 2 teaspoons of salt.
12. In a second shallow bowl, beat the eggs.
13. In a third shallow bowl, place the breadcrumbs.
14. Remove the chicken breast balls from plastic wrap.
15. Coat each chicken breast ball with flour mixture, then dip into beaten eggs and finally coat with breadcrumbs and cayenne pepper.
16. Arrange the breaded chicken balls onto a plate.
17. With plastic wrap, cover the plate and freeze for about 15 minutes.
18. Preheat oven to 400°F (204°C).
19. Line a baking sheet with a piece of foil.
20. In a large, deep skillet, heat the oil over medium heat and cook the chicken balls for about 1 minute per side.
21. With a slotted spoon, transfer the chicken balls onto the prepared baking sheet.
22. Sprinkle the chicken balls with salt and cayenne pepper.

23. Bake for about 15-17 minutes.
24. Remove the baking sheet from the oven and set it aside for about 5 minutes before serving.

Chicken Paprika

Your family might still be using this recipe from the 1960s, but we'll include it here in case you haven't tried it. It's easy and delicious.

Serves 4 | Prep. time 10 min. | Cooking time 1 hour, 15 min.

Ingredients

2 tablespoons bacon grease
1 tablespoon butter
2 medium onions, chopped
1 ½ cups beef broth
1 tablespoon paprika
1 fryer chicken, cut into pieces
1 cup sour cream

Hot rice or pasta, for serving

Directions

1. In a deep skillet with a lid, heat the bacon grease and butter. Brown the onions and chicken. Add the broth and paprika. Bring it to a boil.
2. Reduce the heat to simmer. Cook for 1 hour, and serve over rice or pasta.

Chicken Fricassee

An English-originated chicken feast that is also popular in France. This festive chicken meal is the best choice for a lavish dinner. This is one of my mom's favorite dishes during the 1960s.

Serves 6 | Prep time 20 minutes | Cooking time 1 hour 20 minutes

Ingredients
Chicken
4 tablespoons butter
1 onion, sliced thinly
1 celery stalk, sliced thinly
1 carrot, sliced thinly
2½-3 pounds chicken, cut into pieces
3 tablespoons flour
½ teaspoon salt
⅛ teaspoon ground white pepper

3 cups chicken broth

1 cup dry white wine

1 small herb bouquet (2 parsley sprigs, ⅓ bay leaf, and ⅛ tsp thyme), tied in washed cheesecloth

Braised onions

18-24 small onions, peeled

½ cup water

2 tablespoons butter

Salt and ground black pepper, as required

1 small herb bouquet (2 parsley sprigs, ⅛ tsp thyme, and ⅓ bay leaf), tied in cheesecloth

Stewed mushrooms

⅓ cup water

1 tablespoon butter

¼ tablespoon fresh lemon juice

Salt, as required

¼ pound fresh mushrooms, sliced

Sauce

½ cup whipping cream

2 egg yolks

2-3 drops fresh lemon juice

Pinch of ground nutmeg

Salt and ground white pepper, as required

Final cooking

1-2 tablespoons butter, softened

¼ cup fresh parsley, chopped

Directions

1. For the chicken, in a heavy-bottomed skillet, melt the butter over medium heat and sauté the onions, celery, and carrots for about 5 minutes.
2. Stir in the chicken and cook for 3-4 minutes.
3. Reduce the heat to low and cook, covered for about 10 minutes, flipping the chicken once.

4. Stir in the flour, salt, and black pepper and cook, covered for about 4 minutes.
5. Add the chicken broth and stir to combine.
6. Stir in the wine and herb bouquet and bring to a boil.
7. Reduce the heat to low and simmer, covered for about 25-30 minutes.
8. Meanwhile, for braised onions: in a saucepan, add all ingredients and bring to a boil.
9. Reduce the heat to low and simmer, covered for about 45-50 minutes.
10. Remove from the heat and discard the herb bouquet.
11. With a slotted spoon, transfer the onion into a bowl, reserving the cooking liquid.
12. For the stewed mushrooms: in a saucepan, add the water, butter, lemon juice, and salt and bring to a boil.
13. Stir in the mushrooms and cook, covered for about 5 minutes, tossing frequently.
14. Remove from the heat and with a slotted spoon, transfer the mushrooms into a bowl, reserving the cooking liquid.
15. For the sauce: in a pan, add the reserved cooking liquids over medium heat and simmer for about 2-3 minutes, skimming off the fat.
16. Increase the heat to medium-high and bring to a boil, stirring frequently.
17. Cook until the liquid reaches 2-2½ cups.
18. Meanwhile, in a bowl, add the cream and egg yolks and beat until well combined.
19. Slowly add the hot sauce into the cream mixture, beating continuously until well combined.
20. Return the sauce into the pan over medium-high heat and bring to a boil, stirring continuously.
21. Stir in the lemon juice, nutmeg, salt, and white pepper and remove from the heat.
22. Through a fine sieve, strain the sauce into a bowl.
23. In a large pan, add the chicken mixture, onions, mushrooms, and sauce over medium heat and bring to a gentle simmer.
24. Cover the pan and simmer for about 5 minutes, basting the

chicken with sauce frequently.
25. Stir in the utter and remove from the heat.
26. Serve hot with the garnishing of parsley.

Chicken and Mushroom Casserole

Casseroles one-pot meals were all the rage in the 1960s and this family recipe is still one of my favorite. Three words perfectly describe this retro casserole —simple, quick, and delicious. Even if you have a picky palate, this chicken casserole won't disappoint you. This is one easy weeknight dinner for the whole family.

Serves 4 | Prep. time 4–10 minutes | Cooking time 46 minutes

Ingredients
½ cup low-sodium chicken broth or water
¼ teaspoon garlic powder
¼ teaspoon pepper

½ teaspoon dried thyme

½ teaspoon salt

1 (10½-ounce) can condensed cream of mushroom soup

½ pound boneless, skinless chicken breasts, diced into bite-sized pieces

½ cup milk

1 cup fresh mushrooms, sliced

1½ cups dry uncooked penne pasta or other cut pasta

½ cup grated mozzarella cheese

¼ cup sour cream

Garnish (optional)

Chopped fresh parsley

Grated parmesan cheese

Directions

1. Preheat the oven to 425°F (218°C). Grease an 8-inch-square baking dish with some cooking spray.
2. Add the milk, chicken broth, condensed soup, salt, thyme, garlic powder, and pepper to a mixing bowl. Mix well.
3. Add the pasta, chicken, and mushrooms.
4. Pour into the baking dish, cover with foil and bake for 35–40 minutes until the pasta is cooked well.
5. Stir; add sour cream and combine well. Top with the mozzarella cheese.
6. Bake for 5 more minutes uncovered until the cheese melts.
7. Serve warm.

Classic Chicken Cacciatora

This retro recipe dates back to 1960. Chicken Cacciatora is also known as "Chicken Hunter Style," which is a translation of the Italian name *pollo alla cacciatora*. It pairs great with rice, spaghetti, or noodles sprinkled with parmesan cheese.

Serves 4 | Prep. time 10 minutes | Cooking time 40 minutes

Ingredients
1 clove garlic
1 teaspoon oregano, crumbled
1 (3–3½-pound) frying chicken, cut into bite-sized pieces
2 tablespoons olive oil
Salt and pepper to taste
1–½ cups mushrooms, sliced
1 (1-pound) can stewed tomatoes

Directions

1. Season the chicken with oregano, salt, and pepper.
2. Heat the olive oil and garlic over medium heat in a medium saucepan or skillet.
3. Add the chicken and stir-cook until evenly brown.
4. Remove the garlic clove; add the mushrooms and stir-cook until evenly brown.
5. Add the stewed tomatoes; cover and simmer for 25–30 minutes.
6. Uncover and cook until the sauce is thickened.
7. Serve with cooked rice or spaghetti.

Salisbury Steak

A classic American dish of beef with mushroom sauce. You can treat your family to this delicious dish using my great-aunt's Eunice foolproof recipe.

Serves 4 | Prep time 15 minutes | Cooking time 3 hours 6 minutes

Ingredients
1 pound lean ground beef
¼ cup milk
¼ cup panko breadcrumbs
1 (1-ounce) packet dry onion soup mix
1 tablespoon olive oil
¾ cup water
2 (10½-ounce) cans condensed cream of mushroom soup, undiluted
1 (1-ounce) packet dry au jus gravy mix
1 (8-ounce) container sliced fresh mushrooms
1 small onion, chopped

Directions

1. In a large bowl, add the beef, milk, breadcrumbs, and onion soup mix and with your hands, mix until well combined.
2. Make 4 equal-sized patties from the mixture.
3. Heat in a large skillet over medium-high heat and cook the patties for about 3 minutes per side.
4. Transfer the patties onto a plate.
5. In a medium bowl, add the water, condensed soup, and dry au jus mix and beat until well combined.
6. In the bottom of a large slow cooker, place onions and mushrooms and arrange the patties on top.
7. Pour the soup mixture on top.
8. Set the slow cooker on "Low" and cook, covered for about 3-4 hours.
9. Serve hot.

Steak Diane

A very popular dish in the early 60s, especially in New York City. It's supposedly named after the Roman goddess Diana.

Serves 4 | Prep time 10 minutes | Cooking time 20 minutes

Ingredients
4 (½-pound) strip steaks, pound into ¼-inch thickness
Salt and ground black pepper, as required
1 teaspoon dry mustard, divided
¼ cup margarine
3 tablespoons fresh lemon juice
1 teaspoon Worcestershire sauce
2 teaspoons fresh chives, minced

Directions

1.   Season each steak with salt and black pepper evenly.

2. Then rub the steaks with ⅛ teaspoon of mustard.
3. Melt the margarine in a large skillet over medium-high heat and cook 2 steaks for about 2-3 minutes per side.
4. With a slotted spoon, transfer the steaks onto a hot plate.
5. Repeat with the remaining steaks.
6. In the same skillet, add the remaining mustard, lemon juice, Worcestershire sauce, and chives and bring to a boil.
7. Stir the steaks into the skillet and cook for about 2-3 minutes.
8. Serve hot.

Beef Wellington

A classic steak dish of English origin that rose into popularity in the US around the 1960s in restaurants and quickly became my aunt Mary's favorite dish. This is her recipe which includes beef tenderloin coated with liver pate and mushroom duxelles and then wrapped in puff pastry. An elegant dish to make on special occasions.

Serves 8 | Prep time 20 minutes | Cooking time 50 minutes

Ingredients
2½ pounds beef tenderloin
4 tablespoons butter, softened and divided
½ cup fresh mushrooms, sliced
1 onion, chopped
2 ounces liver pate

Salt and ground black pepper, as required
1 (17½-ounce) package frozen puff pastry, thawed
1 egg yolk, beaten
1 (10½-ounce) can beef broth
2 tablespoons red wine

Directions

1. Preheat your oven to 450°F (232°C).
2. Coat the beef tenderloin with 2 tablespoons of butter.
3. Arrange the beef tenderloin onto a baking sheet and bake for about 10-15 minutes or until browned.
4. Remove the beef tenderloin from the oven and set aside to cool completely.
5. Reserve the pan juices.
6. Melt 2 tablespoons of butter in a skillet over medium heat and sauté the mushrooms and onion for about 5 minutes.
7. Remove the mushroom mixture from heat and set aside to cool.
8. In a bowl, add remaining butter, pate, salt, and black pepper and mix well.
9. Spread pate mixture over beef and top with mushroom mixture.
10. With your hands, roll out the puff pastry dough.
11. Place the beef in the center of rolled dough.
12. Fold up, and seal all the edges.
13. Arrange the beef in a 9x13-inch baking dish.
14. With a knife, cut a few slits in the top of the dough, and brush with beaten egg yolk.
15. Bake for about 10 minutes.
16. Now set the temperature of the oven to 425°F (218°C).
17. Bake for about 10-15 minutes or until pastry is golden brown.
18. Remove from the oven and set aside.
19. In a small saucepan, place the reserved beef juices, broth, and wine over high heat and bring to a boil, stirring occasionally.
20. Cook for about 10-15 minutes or until slightly reduced.
21. Remove from the heat and strain the broth mixture.
22. Serve the beef wellington with a broth mixture.

Stuffed Bacon Meatloaf

A meaty treat that became a quintessential dish in America during the 1960s and still is nowadays.

Serves 4 / Prep time 20 minutes / Cooking time 1 hour 17 minutes

Ingredients
2 tablespoons vegetable oil
½ medium onion, diced
1 carrot, peeled and finely diced
½ red bell pepper, diced thin
2 garlic cloves, minced
1 pound ground meat mix of beef, pork, veal
¼ cup breadcrumbs
1 large egg
2 tablespoons tomato sauce
2 tablespoons Worcestershire sauce

1 tablespoon dried parsley
1 teaspoon garlic powder
1 teaspoon sea salt
½ teaspoon ground black pepper
4 mozzarella string cheese sticks
6 bacon strips, more if needed
2 tablespoons ketchup

Directions

1. Preheat the oven to 375°F (191°C).
2. In a large skillet, warm the oil over medium heat. Add the onions, carrots and pepper and sauté for about 5 minutes.
3. Add the garlic and sauté for about 1 minute.
4. Remove the skillet from heat and with a slotted spoon, transfer the onion mixture into a bowl. Let cool for 5 minutes
5. In a large bowl, add the meatloaf mix, onion mixture, breadcrumbs, egg, tomato sauce, Worcestershire sauce, parsley, garlic powder, salt, and black pepper and mix until well combined.
6. Divide the meat mixture into 2 parts and pat it into ½-inch thickness.
7. Place 2 string cheese sticks in the middle of each meat mixture and then each ones into loaves.f
8. Brush the ketchup on the outside each loaf. Roll the bacon strips around each loaf. Secure with toothpicks if needed.
9. Place into a casserole or baking dish and bake for about 50-60 minutes.
10. Remove from the oven and set aside to cool for about 10 minutes before slicing.
11. Cut into desired-sized slices and serve.

Beef Burgundy with Noodles

An American take on the French dish beef bourguignon that became very popular in the 1960s. Chunks of beef sirloin are simmered in mushroom and Burgundy sauce and then served over egg noodles.

Serves 2 | Prep time 15 minutes | Cooking time 1 hour 10 minutes

Ingredients
2 teaspoons butter
½ pound beef top sirloin steak, cut into ¼-inch-thick strips
2 tablespoons onion, chopped
1½ cups fresh mushrooms, quartered
¾ cup Burgundy wine
¼ cup plus 2 tablespoons water, divided
3 tablespoons fresh parsley, minced and divided
1 bay leaf
1 whole clove

¼ teaspoon salt
⅛ teaspoon pepper
4 ounces uncooked medium egg noodles
1 tablespoon all-purpose flour

Directions

1. In a Dutch oven, melt butter over medium-high heat and cook the beef and onion for about 1-2 minutes, stirring continuously.
2. Stir in mushrooms, wine, ¼ cup of water, 2 tablespoons parsley, and seasonings; bring to a boil.
3. Reduce the heat to low and simmer, covered for about 1 hour.
4. Meanwhile, cook egg noodles according to package directions.
5. Drain the noodles completely.
6. In a small bowl, add the flour and remaining water and mix until smooth.
7. Add the flour mixture into the beef mixture and bring to a boil, stirring frequently.
8. Cook for about 2 minutes or until thickened, stirring continuously.
9. Discard bay leaf and clove.
10. Divide the noodles onto serving plates and serve with the topping of the beef mixture.

Chicken Liver Stroganoff

This is another chicken classic from the great 1960s: chicken livers cooked to a perfect creamy texture in sour cream and butter. Tastes great with cooked rice or mashed potatoes to make one fulfilling meal.

Serves 4 | Prep. time 10 minutes | Cooking time 22 minutes

Ingredients
½ pound chicken livers, halved
1 cup thinly sliced onions
1 cup button mushrooms, quartered
¼ cup butter or margarine, melted
½ teaspoon salt
Dash black pepper
1 tablespoon paprika
1 cup dairy sour cream

Hot cooked rice or mashed potatoes to serve

Directions

1. Heat the butter over medium heat in a medium saucepan or skillet.
2. Add the onion and stir-cook until softened and translucent, about 2 minutes.
3. Season the livers with paprika, salt and pepper. Add them to the pan along with the mushrooms and stir-cook until evenly brown.
4. Cover and simmer over low heat for about 10 minutes, until the livers are tender.
5. Add the sour cream; stir-cook for another 10 minutes.
6. Serve warm with some cooked rice or mashed potatoes. Garnish with parsley (optional).

Meatball Stroganoff

A Russian dish of beef that has become popular in the US during the 60s, thanks to manufacturers making beef stroganoff mixes. Surely your kids would love to enjoy this everyday meal.

Serves 4 | Prep time 15 minutes | Cooking time 20 minutes

Ingredients
1 tablespoon olive oil
1 (12-ounce) package frozen fully-cooked Italian meatballs, thawed
1½ cups beef broth
1 teaspoon dried parsley flakes
¾ teaspoon dried basil
½ teaspoon dried oregano
½ teaspoon salt
¼ teaspoon ground black pepper
1 cup heavy whipping cream

¾ cup sour cream

Directions

1. In a large skillet, heat oil over medium-high heat and cook the meatballs for about 5 minutes or until browned.
2. With a slotted spoon, transfer the meatballs onto a plate.
3. In the skillet, add the broth and with a spoon, stir to loosen the browned bits from the bottom.
4. Stir in the herbs, salt, and black pepper and bring to a boil.
5. Cook for about 5-7 minutes or until liquid is reduced to ½ cup.
6. Add meatballs, noodles, and whipping cream and bring to a boil.
7. Reduce the heat to low and simmer, covered for about 3-5 minutes.
8. Stir in sour cream and cook for about 2-3 minutes
9. Serve hot.

Swedish Meatballs

This recipe of iconic and delicious meatballs with gravy is my father's favorite childhood dish. He always says grandma made the best Swedish Meatballs! Here is his recipe.

Serves 6 | Prep time 20 minutes | Cooking time 30 minutes

Ingredients

1⅔ cups evaporated milk, divided
⅔ cup onion, chopped
¼ cup fine dry breadcrumbs
½ teaspoon ground allspice
½ teaspoon salt
Pinch of ground black pepper
1 pound lean ground beef
2 teaspoons butter
2 teaspoons beef bouillon granules
1 cup boiling water
2 tablespoons all-purpose flour
½ cup cold water
1 tablespoon fresh lemon juice

Directions

1. In a bowl, add ⅔ cup of evaporated milk, onion, breadcrumbs, allspice, salt, and black pepper, and mix until well combined.
2. Add the beef and gently stir to combine.
3. Refrigerate to chill.
4. With wet hands, make about 1-inch balls from the mixture.
5. In a large skillet, melt butter over medium heat and cook the meatballs for about 5 minutes or until browned.
6. Meanwhile, in a small bowl, dissolve the bouillon in boiling water.
7. Place the bouillon mixture over meatballs and bring to a boil.
8. Cover the skillet and simmer for about 15 minutes.
9. Meanwhile, dissolve the flour in cold water.
10. With a slotted spoon, transfer the meatballs onto a plate.
11. Skim the fat from pan juices.
12. Add flour mixture and remaining evaporated milk into the pan juices and stir to combine.
13. Place the pan over low heat and cook until sauce thickens, stirring continuously.
14. Stir in the cooked meatballs and lemon juice and cook for about 1-2 minutes.
15. Serve hot.

Stuffed Florentine Meatloaf

This retro old-school meatloaf recipe is from the 1960s. When people wanted to try something new for dinner, they would find new ways to jazz up a meatloaf. This one has a stuffing of spinach and mozzarella. It delights and surprises your taste buds at the same time.

Serves 8-10 | Prep. time 10 minutes | Cooking time 60 minutes

Ingredients
Cooking spray
Tomato sauce for serving

Meat Mixture
1 pound ground pork
2 pounds ground beef
1 pound ground veal
3 eggs, slightly beaten

1 teaspoon pepper

2 teaspoons salt

1 teaspoon ground allspice

½ teaspoon dry oregano

1 teaspoon dry basil

1 cup tomato juice

Stuffing

4 green onions, chopped

2 cups frozen chopped spinach, drained

¼ pound deli ham sliced thin, about 8-10 slices

2 ½ cups shredded mozzarella cheese

⅓ cup butter or margarine, melted

Directions

1. Preheat the oven to 325°F (163°C). Grease a baking sheet with some cooking spray.
2. Add the meat mixture ingredients to a mixing bowl. Mix well.
3. Divide into two parts and shape each part into an 11×9-inch rectangle.
4. Arrange in the middle of each rectangle, half of the ham slices. Spread half of the spinach and green onions, and top with half of the cheese. Repeat with the second meatloaf rectangle with the remaining stuffing ingredient
5. Shape into rounded oblong loaves. Brush the top of each meatloaf with the melted butter.
6. Place the loaves in the baking dish and bake for 60 minutes until golden brown.
7. Transfer the loaves to serving plates.
8. Let rest 10-15 minutes before slicing. Serve with some tomato sauce on the side if desired

Zucchini Hamburger Pie

A culinary icon recipe that became popular in America during the 60s. Your family and guests will always enjoy the idea of having this pie for supper!

Serves 8 | Prep time 15 minutes | Cooking time 1 hour 10 minutes

Ingredients
½ pound ground beef
¼ cup onion, chopped finely
1 teaspoon salt
½ teaspoon garlic salt
½ cup green pepper, seeded and chopped
½ cup dry breadcrumbs
¼ cup Parmesan cheese, grated
1 large egg, lightly beaten
1 teaspoon dried parsley flakes
1 teaspoon dried oregano

Double crust pie dough
4 cups zucchini, sliced and divided
2 medium tomatoes, peeled and sliced thinly

Directions

1. Preheat your oven to 350°F (177°C).
2. Heat a non-stick skillet over medium heat and cook the beef, onion, salt, and garlic salt for about 6-8 minutes.
3. Drain the grease from the skillet.
4. Add the green pepper, breadcrumbs, cheese, egg, and herbs and stir to combine.
5. Remove from the heat and set aside.
6. Arrange the bottom pastry on a pie plate.
7. Place 2 cups of zucchini over the bottom crust and top with beef mixture, followed by tomato slices and remaining zucchini.
8. Cover with the top pastry evenly.
9. With a knife, cut a few slits in the top of the pastry.
10. Bake for about 1 hour.
11. Remove from the oven and set aside for about 5 minutes before serving.

Sloppy Joes

A meat recipe that's popular in the Midwest region of the United States. These sloppy joes are made with ground beef, onion, and bell peppers that are simmered in brown sugar and ketchup gravy. It's our family's recipe.

Serves 6 | Prep time 10 minutes | Cooking time 40 minutes

Ingredients
1 pound lean ground beef
¼ cup green bell pepper, seeded and chopped
¼ cup onion, chopped
¾ cup ketchup
3 teaspoons brown sugar
1 teaspoon prepared yellow mustard
½ teaspoon garlic powder
Salt and ground black pepper, as required

Directions

1. Heat a medium skillet over medium heat and cook the ground beef, bell pepper, and onion for about 6-8 minutes.
2. Drain the grease from the beef mixture.
3. Add the remaining ingredients and stir to combine.
4. Reduce the heat to low and simmer for about 30 minutes.
5. Serve hot.

Pâté Chinois

Growing up, pâté chinois was my mom go-to recipe. It's close to being a Shepherd's pie or a cottage pie. She used to make it weekly with left over mashed potatoes and often grind her own left-over beef roast. But it's as good made with regular ground beef. A family favorite to make again and again with plenty of ketchup!

Serves 6 | Prep. time 10 minutes | Cooking time 26 minutes

Ingredients

4 tablespoons butter, divided
1 pound ground beef
Salt and pepper
½ teaspoon garlic powder
1 medium-size onion, chopped

1 can (16 or 17 ounces) cream-style corn
3 cups mashed potatoes
Ketchup for serving
Cooked peas for serving

Directions

1. Preheat the oven to 350°F (177°C) and place the oven rack in the middle position.

2. Warm half of the butter over medium heat in an oven-safe skillet like a large cast iron p. Brown the ground beef until cooked through, about 8-10 minutes taking care of breaking up any lumps. Drain juices out of the pan, season to taste with the garlic powder, salt and black pepper, stir to combine, and set aside.

3. Spread the corn over the ground beef evenly. And then, do the same with the mashed potatoes.

4. Cut the remaining butter into small dices. Dot the potatoes with the diced butter.

5. Bake in the oven, uncovered for 20-25 minutes until golden.

6. Let rest 5-10 minutes before serving with some ketchup and some cooked peas, if desired.

Meat Lasagna

This is perhaps one of my most treasured family recipes. I always cook this whenever I miss my grandmother. It's so deliciously meaty and surprisingly easy to make.

Serves 12 | Prep time 20 minutes | Cooking time 2 hours 40 minutes

Ingredients
¾ pound ground beef
½ pound pepperoni sausage, chopped
½ pound salami, chopped
1 onion, minced
2 (14½-ounce) cans stewed tomatoes
16 ounces tomato sauce
6 ounces tomato paste
1 teaspoon dried oregano
1 teaspoon garlic powder

½ teaspoon salt

¼ teaspoon ground black pepper

9 lasagna noodles

4 cups mozzarella cheese, shredded

2 cups cottage cheese

9 white American cheese slices

12 teaspoons Parmesan cheese, grated

Directions

1. Heat a large skillet over medium heat and cook the ground beef, sausage, salami, and onion for about 7-10 minutes.
2. Drain the grease from the skillet and transfer the meat mixture into a slow cooker.
3. Add the tomatoes, tomato sauce, tomato paste, oregano, garlic powder, salt, and black pepper, and stir to combine.
4. Set the slow cooker on "Low" and cook, covered for about 2 hours.
5. Meanwhile, in a large pan of lightly salted boiling water, cook the lasagna noodles for about 8 minutes or according to the package's directions.
6. Drain the noodles completely.
7. Preheat oven to 350°F (177°C).
8. In the bottom of a baking dish, spread a thin layer of meat mixture.
9. Arrange about ⅓ of the noodles over the meat mixture and top with 1⅓ cups of mozzarella cheese, followed by ⅔ cup of cottage cheese, 3 American cheese slices, and 4 teaspoons of Parmesan cheese.
10. Spread about ⅓ of the meat mixture over the cheese layer.
11. Repeat the layers twice.
12. Bake for about 30 minutes or until cheese is melted.
13. Remove from the oven and set aside for about 10minutes before serving.

Beefy Spanish Rice

With the popularity and convenience of canned foods in the 1960s, this vintage Spanish rice meal is prepared from ground beef and Campbell's Tomato Soup. It`s quick and wholesome, perfect for a weeknight dinner.

Serves 4 | Prep. time 10 minutes | Cooking time 20–25 minutes

Ingredients
½ cup chopped onion
1 pound ground beef
1 cup water
½ cup quick-cooking rice, uncooked
⅓ cup green pepper, chopped
1 large clove garlic, minced
2 teaspoons Worcestershire sauce
½ teaspoon salt

1 (10¾-ounce) can Campbell's Tomato Soup
Pinch of pepper

Directions

1. Grease a medium saucepan or skillet with cooking spray and heat it over medium heat.
2. Add the onion, green pepper, and garlic; stir-cook until the onion softens.
3. Add the beef and stir-cook until evenly brown. Remove the excess fat.
4. Add the other ingredients and stir.
5. Bring to a boil.
6. Cover and simmer over low heat for about 15 minutes, until the rice is tender.
7. Serve warm.

Maple-Glazed Baked Ham

The mouthwatering combination of ham and maple makes this 1960s vintage recipe a party favorite. It's party time with your favorite boneless ham with a yummy maple twist!

Serves 18–20 | Prep time 30 minutes
Cooking time 3 hours 20 minutes

Ingredients

¾ cup light-brown sugar, firmly packed
1 cup dark corn syrup
1 boneless ham, fully cooked, about 8–10 pound
Whole cloves
2 tablespoons prepared mustard
1 tablespoon maple flavoring

Directions

1. Preheat the oven to 325°F (163°C).
2. Add the ham, fat side up, to a shallow roasting pan. Insert a thermometer in the ham.
3. Bake until the thermometer reads 130°F (55°C), about 2½–3 hours.
4. Remove the ham from the oven, remove the thermometer, and finally remove the ham rind.
5. Make diamond-shaped cuts in the ham fat and place a clove in each diamond shape.
6. In order to glaze, increase the oven temperature to 450°F (232°C).
7. Combine all the remaining ingredients in a mixing bowl.
8. Spread half the glaze over the ham; bake for 10 minutes.
9. Spread remaining glaze and bake for 10 more minutes.
10. Serve warm.

Sautéed Calf's Liver

A usual choice for a meal in the United Kingdom. It had widespread popularity in America around the 20th century, especially in the1960s, and can be found in retro American home-style diner menus. I found this recipe from my grandmother's recipe box. This simple dish consists of tender liver slices sautéed in butter.

Serves 4 | Prep time 15 minutes | Cooking time 4 minutes

Ingredients
1 pound calf's liver, cut into ½-inch thick slices
1 large onion, thinly sliced
Salt and ground black pepper, as required
½ cup flour
3 tablespoons butter
1 large onion, sliced

Directions

1. Season the liver with salt and black pepper evenly.
2. In a skillet, sauté the onions until brown. Remove from heat and set aside.
3. Then lightly coat the liver slices with flour, shaking off excess.
4. In a frying pan, melt butter over high heat and sauté the calf slices for about 1-2 minutes per side.
5. Top the onions over the sautéed liver and mix. Serve hot.

Slow-Cooked Baked Beans and Sausages

This dish is a combo of pork sausage, a different variety of beans, tomatoes, and barbecue sauce. We used to eat this a lot when I was growing up and I still make it for my family as an easy everyday dinner. We make it in the slow cooker as it cooks all day and fills the house with delicious aromas.

Serves 16 | Prep time 15 minutes | Cooking time 8 hours 10 minutes

Ingredients
1 pound bulk spicy pork sausage
1 medium onion, chopped
2 (15-ounce) cans pork and beans
1 (16-ounce) can butter beans, rinsed and drained
1 (16-ounce) can kidney beans, rinsed and drained
1 (15½-ounce) can navy beans, rinsed and drained
1 (15-ounces) can black beans, rinsed and drained
1 (10-ounces) can diced tomatoes and green chilies, drained
½ cup ketchup
½ cup hickory smoke-flavored barbecue sauce
½ cup brown sugar
1 teaspoon liquid smoke
1 teaspoon ground mustard
1 teaspoon steak seasoning

Directions

1. Heat a large non-stick skillet over medium heat and cook the sausage and onion for about 8-10 minutes.
2. Remove from the heat and drain the grease completely.
3. In a slow cooker, add the sausage mixture and remaining ingredients and stir to combine.
4. Set the slow cooker on "Low" and cook, covered for about 7-8 hours.
5. Serve hot.

Tuna and Noodles Casserole

An American household meal, especially in the 60s, this casserole is a combo of tuna, peas, cream of mushroom soup, milk, and butter.

Serves 6 | Prep time 15 minutes | Cooking time 35 minutes

Ingredients
Non-stick cooking spray
2 cups dry egg noodles
1 (15-ounce) can low-sodium peas, drained
1 (10½-ounce) can cream of mushroom soup
1 (12-ounce) can light tuna in water, drained
1 cup whole milk
⅓ cup dry breadcrumbs
2 tablespoons butter, melted
Salt and ground black pepper, as required

Directions

1. Preheat your oven to 400°F (204°C).
2. Grease a baking dish with cooking spray.
3. In a large pan of lightly salted boiling water, cook the noodles for about 8-10 minutes or according to the package's directions.
4. Drain the noodles completely.
5. In a large bowl, add the cooked noodles, peas, soup, tuna, and milk and mix well.
6. Place the tuna mixture into the prepared casserole dish.
7. Bake for about 20 minutes.
8. In a small bowl, mix the breadcrumbs and melted butter.
9. Remove the casserole dish from the oven and sprinkle with the breadcrumb mixture evenly.
10. Bake for about 5 minutes.
11. Remove from the oven and set aside for about 5 minutes.
12. Sprinkle with salt and black pepper and serve.

Scallops with Wine, Garlic, and Herbs

A French-inspired classic seafood choice for dinner. Scallops are prepared with a sauce of wine, herbs, and garlic and were very popular in the 50s and 60s. Whenever there were scallops available, this was my Aunt Eunice's recipe of choice to cook.

Serves 4 | Prep time 15 minutes | Cooking time 17 minutes

Ingredients
3 tablespoons butter, divided
⅓ cup yellow onions, minced
1½ tablespoons shallot, minced
1 garlic clove, minced
1½ pounds scallops
Salt and ground black pepper, as required
1 tablespoon olive oil
⅔ cup dry white wine

1 bay leaf
⅛ teaspoon dried thyme
¼ cup Swiss cheese, grated
2 tablespoons butter, cut into 6 pieces

Directions

1. In a small saucepan, melt 1 tablespoon of butter over medium heat and sauté the onion for about 3-4 minutes.
2. Stir in the shallots and garlic and sauté for about 1 minute.
3. Remove from the heat and set aside.
4. Season the scallops with salt and black pepper and then coat with flour, shaking off excess.
5. In a skillet, heat oil and remaining butter over medium heat and sauté the scallops for about 2 minutes.
6. Stir in the wine, bay leaf, thyme, and cooked onion mixture and cook, covered for about 5 minutes.
7. Uncover and cook for about 1 minute.
8. Remove from the heat and discard bay leaf.
9. Transfer the scallops into Pyrex dishes evenly and top with cheese and butter.
10. Set the oven to broiler.
11. Broil the Pyrex dishes for about 3-4 minutes.
12. Serve hot.

Steamed Mussels

This elegant dish of mussels is steamed in white wine with a parsley twist, and one of my mother's favorite childhood recipes.

Serves 6 | Prep time 20 minutes | Cooking time 13 minutes

Ingredients
2 cups dry white wine
6 tablespoons butter
½ cup shallots, minced
8 parsley sprigs
¼ teaspoon dried thyme
½ bay leaf
⅛ teaspoon ground black pepper
3-4 pounds mussels, scrubbed
½ cup fresh parsley, chopped
Directions

1. In a large pan, add the wine, butter, shallot, parsley sprigs, thyme, bay leaf, and black pepper, and ring to a boil.
2. Boil for about 2-3 minutes.
3. Add the mussels and cook, covered for about 5 minutes.
4. Remove from the heat and discard any unopened mussels.
5. Serve hot with the topping of chopped parsley.

Oven Crusty Fish

This crunchy fish treat comes all the way from 1967, but it can still come fresh from your oven! Cornflakes add the crispiness, and it's delightful paired with Tabasco sauce. If you prefer your fish tangy, serve it with some lemon wedges.

Serves 6 | Prep. time 15 minutes | Cooking time 30 minutes

Ingredients
¾ teaspoon Tabasco sauce
½ teaspoon salt
1 egg
1 tablespoon water
1½ pounds fish fillets (flounder, cod, haddock etc.), fresh or frozen and thawed
2 tablespoons melted butter or vegetable oil

1 cup cornflake crumbs
Lemon wedges
Finely chopped parsley

Directions

1. Combine the eggs, salt and Tabasco in a medium-large bowl. Beat well.
2. Coat the fish evenly with the egg mixture, then with the cornflake crumbs.
3. Preheat the oven to 375°F (191°C). Grease a baking sheet with cooking spray or melted butter.
4. Place the fish over the sheet and top with the melted butter.
5. Bake for about 20–30 minutes until cooked well and crisped.
6. Serve with some lemon wedges.

VEGETARIAN RECIPES

Waldorf Salad

A salad that became a staple dish in America during the 1960s. This salad contains apples, grapes, and walnuts with a creamy dressing. You can make it in a few minutes

Serves 4 | Prep time 15-20 minutes

Ingredients
Dressing
2 tablespoons apple cider vinegar
2 tablespoons half and half cream
¾ cup mayonnaise
Salt and ground black pepper, to taste

Salad
3-4 crisp apples, cord, and chopped
8 ounces red seedless grapes, sliced
1 cup sliced celery
¾ cup walnuts, chopped
Lettuce leaves for serving

Directions

1. For the dressing: add all ingredients to a bowl and whisk until well combined and smooth.
2. Transfer the dressing into a salad bowl.
3. Add the apples, grapes, walnuts, and celery and stir to combine.
4. Serve the salad on a bed of fresh lettuce leaves.

Potato Salad

A classic potato salad dressing that combines buttermilk, mayonnaise, vinegar, Dijon mustard, and seasoning to highlights the flavors of potatoes. This is my grandma's recipe, which I've made so many times. It is always an instant hit to every potluck I bring this to. You can substitute different mustard types to add different flavor profiles.

Serves 6 | Prep time 15 minutes | Cooking time 10-15 minutes

Ingredients
2 pounds white russet potatoes, peeled
¾ cup celery, chopped
2-3 green onions, sliced
1 large kosher dill pickle, diced

Dressing
2 tablespoons white vinegar

¾ cup mayonnaise
¼ cup buttermilk
1 tablespoon Dijon mustard
½ teaspoon celery seeds
1 tablespoon white sugar
Salt and ground black pepper, as required

Directions

1. In a large pan of boiling water, cook the potatoes for about 10-15 minutes or until fork-tender but still have a bit to them.
2. Through a colander, drain the potatoes.
3. Cover the colander with a clean kitchen towel for about 15 minutes.
4. Uncover the potatoes and set them aside to cool for about 15 minutes.
5. After cooling, cut the potatoes into bite-sized pieces.
6. While the potatoes are cooling, prepare the dressing. Add all the ingredients to a salad bowl and whisk until smooth and sugar has dissolved.
7. Add the celery, green onions, and pickle. Stir to coat.
8. Gently fold in the cooled potatoes.
9. Refrigerate to chill before serving.

Leek and Potato Soup

This potato soup became a staple dish in every American household in the 1960s, including my Aunt Eunice's. She said this recipe came from her father's grandmother. This classically creamy soup is a flavorful combo of potato, leek, and cream.

Serves 8 | Prep time 15 minutes | Cooking time 55 minutes

Ingredients
1 pound potatoes, peeled and chopped
1 pound leeks, sliced thinly
8 cups water
1 tablespoon salt
4-6 tablespoons whipping cream
2-3 tablespoons fresh parsley, minced

Directions

1. In a pan, add all ingredients except for cream and parsley over medium-high heat and bring to a boil.
2. Reduce the heat to medium-low and simmer, partially covered for about 40-50 minutes.
3. Remove from the heat and stir in the cream.
4. With an immersion blender, blend the soup until smooth.
5. Serve hot with the garnishing of parsley.

Cream of Mushroom Soup

An American soup that is inspired by Italian and French creamy sauces and soups, especially made popular by Campbell's in the 1960s. This recipe is my grandmother's version and has mushrooms, tarragon, milk, cream, and chicken broth that complement each other nicely.

Serves 6 | Prep time 15 minutes | Cooking time 30 minutes

Ingredients
4 tablespoons butter
1 cup onion, minced
¼ cup flour
1 cup hot chicken broth
6 cups milk
4 cups fresh mushrooms, sliced
¼ teaspoon dried tarragon leaves
½ cup heavy cream

Salt and ground white pepper, as required
1 teaspoon fresh lemon juice

Directions

1. In a heavy-bottomed saucepan, melt the butter over medium heat and cook the onion for about 7-8 minutes, stirring frequently.
2. Stir in the flour and cook for about 2-3 minutes, stirring continuously.
3. Slowly, add in the broth, beating continuously, and bring to a boil.
4. Add the milk and beat until well combined.
5. Stir in the mushrooms and tarragon and simmer for about 20 minutes, stirring frequently.
6. Stir in the cream and simmer for about 2-3 minutes.
7. Stir in the salt, black pepper, and lemon juice and remove from the heat.
8. Serve hot.

Mashed Potatoes

A very popular side dish in every American household from the 60s until today. These creamy mashed potatoes will be a hit for any meat dish.

Serves 6 | Prep time 15 minutes | Cooking time 116 minutes

Ingredients
4-5 large baking potatoes, peeled and quartered
¼-½ cup warm milk
2 tablespoons butter, softened
1-2 teaspoon fresh chiseled chives (optional)
Salt and white pepper, to taste

Directions

1. In a large pan of salted boiling water, cook the potatoes for about 10-15 minutes.
2. Drain the water and place the pan of potatoes over medium heat

for bout 1 minute, tossing continuously.

3. Remove from the heat and with a potato masher, mash the potatoes.

4. Add the milk and beat the potatoes with a hand-held mixer until desired consistency is achieved, about 1-3 minutes on medium speed.

5. Season with salt and pepper to taste. Add chives, if using, and stir to combine.

6. Serve warm.

Braised Dill Potatoes

This is one of my mother's favorite potato dishes, and I'm forever grateful she passed down her recipe to me. These potatoes are flavored with butter, dill, and chicken broth.

Serves 4 | Prep time 15 minutes | Cooking time 25 minutes

Ingredients

1 pound baby or fingerling potatoes
1 cup chicken broth
1 tablespoon butter
3 tablespoons fresh dill, snipped
Salt and freshly ground black pepper, to taste

Directions

1. In a large saucepan, add the potatoes, broth, and butter over medium-high heat and cook, covered for about 12 minutes.

2.   Uncover and cook for about 7-10 minutes or until all the liquid is absorbed.
3.   Sprinkle with dill and season with salt and black pepper to taste. Cook for about 2-3 minutes.
4.   Serve hot.

Sautéed Mushrooms

A favorite side dish recipe in the 1960s. This quick and easy mushroom recipe makes a perfect side dish.

Serves 2 | Prep time 10 minutes | Cooking time 8 minutes

Ingredients
2 tablespoons butter
1 tablespoon olive oil
½ pound fresh mushrooms, sliced or quartered if large
1-2 tablespoons shallots, minced
Salt and ground black pepper, to taste

Directions

1. In a skillet, heat the butter and oil over high heat and cook the mushrooms for about 5-6 minutes, stirring frequently.

2. Add the shallots and stir to combine.
3. Reduce the heat to medium and sauté for about 2 minutes.
4. Season with salt and black pepper to taste and serve hot.

Mushroom and Leek Strudel

An Eastern European treat of pastry that became popular in the 1960s. This pastry is packed with a flavorsome filling of mushrooms, leek, wine, cream, and seasoning. I really love this recipe version that came from my grandmother.

Serves 24 | Prep time 20 minutes | Cooking time 34 minutes

Ingredients
2 tablespoons butter, divided
2 pounds fresh mushrooms, chopped finely and divided
1 medium leek (white portion only), chopped and divided
2 garlic cloves, minced
¼ cup heavy whipping cream
¼ cup white wine
2 tablespoons fresh parsley, minced

1 tablespoon fresh thyme, minced
½ teaspoon salt
¼ teaspoon ground black pepper
12 (14x9-inch) phyllo dough sheets
¾ cup butter, melted
4 tablespoons Parmesan cheese, grated and divided

Directions

1. In a large skillet, melt 1 tablespoon butter over medium-high heat and cook half of the mushrooms, and leek for about 4-5 minutes.
2. Transfer the mushroom mixture into a bowl.
3. In the same skillet, melt the remaining butter over medium-high heat and cook the remaining mushrooms, and leek for about 3-4 minutes.
4. Add the garlic and cook for about 1 minute.
5. Stir in the remaining cooked mushroom mixture, cream, and wine and cook for about 1-2 minutes or until liquid is almost evaporated.
6. Stir in herbs, salt, and black pepper and remove from the heat.
7. Set aside to cool completely.
8. Preheat oven to 375°F (191°C).
9. Line a 15x10x1-inch baking dish with parchment paper.
10. Place 1 phyllo dough sheet onto a smooth surface and brush with butter.
11. Layer with 5 more phyllo sheets, brushing each layer with butter.
12. Spoon half of the mushroom mixture on the center third of phyllo dough to within 1-inch of ends.
13. Sprinkle the top with 2 tablespoons of cheese.
14. Fold up the short sides to seal the filling.
15. Starting with a long side, roll up in jelly-roll style.
16. Arrange the roll into the prepared baking dish, seam side down and brush with butter.
17. Repeat with remaining phyllo sheets and filling mixture.
18. Bake for about 18-22 minutes or until golden brown.
19. Remove from the oven ad set aside for about 10 minutes before serving.

Spanakopita

A favorite Greek savory spinach pie recipe. It became popular with Greek immigrants to America in the 1960s and remains a favorite today. This recipe comes from one of our neighbors when I was growing up and is well worth making for your family, especially to get the kids eating spinach!

Serves 6 | Prep time 20 minutes | Cooking time 1 hour 2 minutes

Ingredients
2 pounds fresh spinach
2 tablespoons fresh parsley, minced
1 teaspoon fresh dill, minced
Salt, as required
2 eggs
½ pound Gruyere cheese, grated
12 phyllo pastry sheets
½ cup butter, melted

Directions

1. Preheat the oven to 350°F (171°C).
2. Grease a 9×9-inch baking dish with cooking spray.
3. Heat a large saucepan over medium-high heat and cook the spinach in 3-4 batches for about 2-3 minutes, stirring frequently.
4. Transfer the spinach onto a baking sheet and set aside to cool.
5. After cooling, squeeze the spinach to remove any excess moisture.
6. Then chop the spinach roughly.
7. In a bowl, add chopped spinach, parsley, dill, and salt and toss to coat well.
8. Add one egg and stir to combine.
9. In another bowl, mix together the cheese and remaining egg.
10. At the bottom of the prepared baking dish, arrange 6 phyllo pastry sheets.
11. Brush each pastry sheet with butter.
12. Place the spinach mixture over pastry sheets and top with cheese mixture.
13. Cover with the remaining phyllo pastry sheets and brush the top with butter.
14. Bake for about 35-40 minutes or until pastry is golden.
15. Remove from the oven and set aside to cool slightly.
16. Carefully flip the side and bake for about 15-20 minutes.
17. Remove from the oven and flip the spanakopita.
18. Cut into squares and serve hot.

SNACKS AND APPETIZER RECIPES

Cheese Biscuits

British-style savory biscuits that are widely popular in the United States. This family recipe of cheddar biscuits is richly flaky and garlicky.

Serves 6 | Prep time 15 minutes | Cooking time 20 minutes

Ingredients
Non-stick cooking spray
3 cups all-purpose flour
3 teaspoons baking powder
1 tablespoon sugar
1 teaspoon salt

¾ teaspoon cream of tartar
½ cup cold butter
1 cup sharp cheddar cheese, shredded
1 garlic clove, minced
¼-½ teaspoon red pepper flakes, crushed
1¼ cups 2% milk

Directions

1. Preheat your oven to 450°F (232°C).
2. Grease a baking sheet with cooking spray.
3. In a large bowl, mix the flour, baking powder, sugar, salt, and cream of tartar.
4. With a pastry blender, cut in the butter until a coarse crumb-like mixture is formed.
5. Add the cheese, garlic, and red pepper flakes and mix until well combined.
6. Add the milk and stir until just moistened.
7. Place about ¼ cupfuls of dough onto the prepared baking sheet about 2-inch apart.
8. Bake for about 18-20 minutes or until golden brown.
9. Serve warm.

Mushroom Turnovers

A recipe of tasty turnovers that was a household staple during my Aunt Eunice's childhood. These flaky, buttery pockets are filled with mushrooms, butter, sour cream, and dill.

Serves 30 | Prep time 25 minutes | Cooking time 22 minutes

Ingredients
Dough
2 (8-ounce) packages cream cheese, softened
1 cup butter, softened
3 cups all-purpose flour

Filling
3 tablespoons butter
½ pound fresh mushrooms, chopped finely
1 large onion, finely chopped

¼ cup sour cream
2 tablespoons all-purpose flour
1 teaspoon snipped fresh dill
1 teaspoon salt
1 large egg, beaten

Directions

1. For the dough: in a large bowl, add the cream cheese and butter and beat until smooth.
2. Slowly add the flour and beat until a dough forms.
3. Divide the dough into 2 portions and shape each into a disk.
4. With plastic wrap, cover each dough disk and refrigerate for about 1 hour.
5. For the filling: in a large skillet, melt butter over medium heat and cook the mushrooms and onion for about 6-8 minutes, stirring frequently.
6. Remove from heat and stir in the sour cream, flour, dill, and salt.
7. Set aside at room temperature to cool completely.
8. Preheat your oven to 400°F (204°C).
9. Place 1 dough disk onto a lightly floured surface and roll into ⅛-inch thickness.
10. Repeat with the remaining dough disk.
11. With a floured 2½-inch round cookie cutter, cut the circles from dough discs.
12. Place about 1 teaspoon of filling on one side of each dough circle.
13. Brush the edges with egg and fold the dough over mushroom filling.
14. With a fork, press the edges to seal.
15. Arrange the turnovers onto an ungreased baking sheet and brush the tops with egg.
16. Bake for about 12-14 minutes or until edges are golden brown.
17. Serve warm.

Stuffed Mushrooms

An Italian-style treat as an appetizer that my grandmother always cooked in the 1960s using her oven range. These baked mushrooms are stuffed with butter, cheese, pecans, breadcrumbs, and seasoning.

Serves 20 | Prep time 15 minutes | Cooking time 23 minutes

Ingredients
Non-stick cooking spray
20 large fresh mushrooms, stems removed
3 tablespoons butter
1 small onion, chopped
¼ cup pecans, chopped finely
¼ cup dry breadcrumbs
3 tablespoons Parmesan cheese, grated
¼ teaspoon dried basil
¼ teaspoon salt

Pinch of cayenne pepper

Directions

1. Preheat your oven to 400°F (204°C).
2. Grease a 15x10x1-inch baking dish with cooking spray.
3. Remove stems from mushrooms and set the caps aside.
4. Then chop the stems finely.
5. In a large skillet, melt butter over medium heat and sauté the chopped mushroom stems and onion for about 5 minutes.
6. Remove from the heat set aside to cool slightly.
7. In a bowl, add the onion mixture and remaining ingredients and stir to combine.
8. Stuff each mushroom cap with a mixture.
9. Arrange the mushroom caps onto the prepared baking sheet.
10. Bake for about 15-18 minutes.
11. Serve warm.

Hot Cheese Canapés

Served piping hot, these canapés are bubbly and scrumptious. They were one of the favorite Christmas appetizers way back in the mid-1960s. They open up a whole new world of retro Christmas feel.

Serves 6 | Prep. time 10 minutes | Cooking time 10 minutes

Ingredients
½ cup mayonnaise
1 cup American cheese, finely shredded
Shrimp or sliced cold cuts
White bread slices, de-crusted and cut into small pieces

Directions

1. Preheat the oven to 350⁰ F (177ºC) and arrange the bread pieces on a baking sheet.
2. Bake in the oven until golden and crispy.
3. Arrange the bread pieces on a baking sheet and top with the shrimp or meat.
4. Add the cheese and mayonnaise to a mixing bowl. Mix well.
5. Spread over the shrimp or meat.
6. Preheat the broiler to medium-high heat.
7. Broil the canapés about 4 inches from the heat source until cheese is melted and bubbly.
8. Serve warm.

Stuffed Cherry Tomatoes

A plate of worth-watching mini treats that rose to popularity in the 1960s.
These cheese-stuffed tomatoes are an excellent fit for any party.

Serves 12 | Prep time 15 minutes

Ingredients
24 cherry tomatoes
3 ounces cream cheese, softened
2 tablespoons mayonnaise
¼ cup cucumber, peeled and chopped finely
1 tablespoon scallion, chopped finely
2 teaspoons fresh dill, minced

Directions

1. Carefully cut a thin slice off the top of each tomato.
2. With a small scooper, scoop out the pulp.

3. Place tomatoes onto paper towels, cut-side-down to drain.
4. In a small bowl, add the cream cheese and mayonnaise and stir until smooth.
5. Add the remaining ingredients and stir to combine.
6. Spoon the cream cheese mixture into tomatoes and refrigerate until serving.

Cocktail Meatballs with Grape Jelly Glaze

A family recipe from the 1960s that will is always a perfect choice for any family, friends gatherings, or potlucks. These cocktail meatballs are simmered in a delicious sauce of grape jelly, chili sauce, and mustard.

Serves 6 | Prep time 15 minutes | Cooking time 1 hour

Ingredients
2 pounds ground beef
10 ounces grape jelly
¼ cup chili sauce
2 tablespoons prepared mustard

Directions

1. Preheat your oven to 350°F (177°C).
2. Line a large baking sheet with a piece of foil.
3. Make golf-sized balls from the beef.

4. Arrange the meatballs onto the prepared roasting pan in a single layer.
5. Bake for about 20-25 minutes or until done completely.
6. Meanwhile, in a Dutch oven, add the jelly, chili sauce, and mustard and cook until just heated.
7. Remove the baking sheet from the oven and drain the meatballs completely.
8. Add the meatballs into the Dutch oven with a jelly mixture and reduce the heat to low.
9. Cover the pan and simmer for about ½ hour.
10. Serve hot.

Fried Shrimp

A recipe of fried shrimp with a Portuguese touch. These fried shrimp are coated in seasoned breadcrumbs, then baked to golden brown perfection. This is also one of my favorite recipes from my Mom's recipe box.

Serves 10 | Prep time 20 minutes | Cooking time 12 minutes

Ingredients
Non-stick cooking spray
1½ cups panko breadcrumbs
1 tablespoon fat-free milk
2 large egg whites
3 tablespoons all-purpose flour
3 teaspoons seafood seasoning
¼ teaspoon salt
¼ teaspoon ground black pepper
30 large shrimp, peeled and deveined

Directions

1. Preheat your oven to 400°F (204°C).
2. Grease a large baking sheet with cooking spray.
3. In a shallow bowl, place the breadcrumbs.
4. In a second shallow bowl, add the milk and egg whites and beat until well combined.
5. In a third shallow bowl, mix the flour, seafood seasoning, salt, and black pepper.
6. Coat the shrimp with flour mixture, then dip into milk mixture and finally coat with breadcrumbs.
7. Arrange the shrimp onto the prepared baking sheet in a single layer.
8. Spray the shrimp with cooking spray.
9. Bake for about 8-12 minutes or until golden brown, flipping once halfway through.
10. Serve warm.

Bacon and Nut-Stuffed Mushroom

This mushroom and bacon recipe ruled during the 60s and 70s. If you're always worrying about how to welcome your guests, this recipe solves your appetizer dilemma! Prepared from fresh mushrooms, this recipe is a sure people pleaser. For the best taste, use white mushrooms with closed, firm caps.

Serves 4 | Prep. time 15 minutes | Cooking time 15 minutes

Ingredients
20 white mushrooms, large enough to be stuffed
1 teaspoon instant minced onions (or 1 tablespoon diced onions)
1 tablespoon lemon juice
½ cup dry breadcrumbs
2 tablespoons butter or margarine, melted
¼ cup sliced Brazil nuts, chopped

1 teaspoon poultry seasoning
2 strips crisp cooked bacon, crumbled
½ teaspoon salt
½ cup chicken stock or water

Directions

1. Preheat the oven to 375°F (191°C).
2. Clean the mushrooms with cold water and dry with a damp cloth. Do not soak.
3. Trim the stems, but do not peel. Reserve the stems and dice them.
4. Brush the mushrooms caps with lemon juice. Set aside.
5. In a mixing bowl, combine 1 teaspoon of water with the instant minced onion; set aside for 5 minutes to soften.
6. Heat the butter over medium heat in a medium saucepan or skillet.
7. Add the minced onion and chopped stems and stir-cook for 3–4 minutes until softened.
8. Add the remaining ingredients and stir cook for a while.
9. Stuff the mixture into the mushroom caps.
10. Place the mushrooms in a greased casserole dish and bake for 10-15 minutes, or until mushrooms are tender and stuffing is golden and crunchy.
11. Serve warm.

Pecan Cheese Balls

You can't call it a party if it does not have these snappy cheese balls. This vintage cheese ball recipe from the 1960s comprises a delicious combination of blue cheese, cheddar cheese, mayonnaise and pecans.

Serves 12 | Prep. time 15 minutes | Chill time 30 minutes

Ingredients

2 ounces blue cheese, at room temperature
½ pound cream cheese, at room temperature
½ cup mayonnaise
½ pound sharp cheddar cheese, shredded
½ teaspoon paprika
½ teaspoon onion, grated
1 cup chopped walnuts or pecans, chopped
Few drops Worcestershire sauce
Crackers for serving

Directions

1. Combine the cheddar, mayonnaise, cream cheese, blue cheese, onion, paprika and half of the nuts in a medium-large bowl.

2. Form into a large cheese ball or two and roll it into the remaining nuts to coat evenly.
3. Refrigerate for 30 minutes and serve with crackers.

Shrimp Cocktail

This is probably one of the most popular hors d'œuvre in America since the 1960s. Shrimps are poached in an aromatic liquid and then served with a cocktail sauce. My grandmother always made it at family gatherings.

Serves 4 | Prep time 20 minutes | Cooking time 25 minutes

Ingredients
Cocktail sauce
½ cup ketchup
¼ cup chili sauce
¼ cup prepared horseradish
1 teaspoon fresh lemon juice
1 teaspoon Worcestershire sauce
3 drops hot sauce
Pinch of salt

For the poaching of shrimp
12 cups cold water
¼ onion, sliced
2 garlic cloves, peeled and bruised
½ of lemon
2 fresh tarragon sprigs
1 bay leaf
1 tablespoon seafood seasoning
1 teaspoon whole black peppercorns
2 pounds shell-on jumbo shrimp, deveined

Directions

1. For the cocktail sauce: in a bowl, add all the ingredients ad mix until well combined.
2. Refrigerate for at least 15 minutes before using.
3. For the poaching liquid: in a pan, add all ingredients except for shrimp over medium heat and bring to a boil.
4. Cook for about 15 minutes.
5. Increase the heat to medium-high and again bring to a rolling boil.
6. Add the shrimp and cook for about 5 minutes.
7. Drain the shrimp and immediately place into a bowl of ice water until cold; drain.
8. Arrange the cold shrimp on a serving platter and serve alongside the cocktail sauce.

Chicken Liver Mousse

A popular appetizer to share. It became popular in the 60s and continues to impress when it's made from scratch and so much tastier than store-bought.

Serves 12 | Prep time 15 minutes | Cooking time 10 minutes

Ingredients
½ cup water
⅓ cup onion, chopped
1 garlic clove, peeled
4 fresh thyme sprigs
4 bay leaves
½ pound chicken livers
1 tablespoon brandy
¼ teaspoon salt
¼ teaspoon ground black pepper
1¼ cups butter, softened

Directions

1. In a large skillet, add the water, onion, garlic, thyme sprigs, and bay leaves over medium heat and bring to a boil.
2. Stir in the chicken livers and cook, uncovered for about 3-5 minutes, stirring frequently.
3. Remove from the heat and set aside, covered for about 5 minutes.
4. Discard bay leaves and thyme sprigs.
5. Drain the liver mixture completely.
6. In a food processor, add the liver mixture, brandy, salt, and black pepper and pulse until livers are chopped roughly.
7. Slowly add butter, 2 tablespoons at a time, and pulse after each addition until smooth.
8. Transfer into a bowl and serve.

Smoked Salmon Mousse

Another popular mousse in the 1960s that was usually served as canapé for the cocktail hour. This flavorful mousse is made with a delicious combo of smoked salmon, cream cheese, heavy cream, lemon juice, and dill.

Serves 16 | Prep time 15 minutes

Ingredients
4 ounces smoked salmon
1 (8-ounce) package cream cheese, softened
2 tablespoons heavy cream
1 tablespoon fresh lemon juice
½ teaspoon dried dill weed
Salt and ground black pepper, as required

Directions

1. In a food processor, add the smoked salmon and pulse until smooth.
2. Add the remaining ingredients and pulse until well combined.
3. Transfer into a serving bowl and serve.

French Onion Soup

Still a favorite in our family for cold winter meals, onion soup can be traced back to the Roman Empire! Onions were cheap and easy to grow. But it's in Paris that this the modern version of the soup was created in the 18th century. It was introduced in America in 1861 by Marie-Julie Mouquin, wife of the famous French restaurateur. It was a very "chic" dish to order at restaurants in the 1960s. Here is our family recipe.

Serves 6 | Prep time 15 minutes | Cook time 1 hour

Ingredients
2 tablespoons butter, plus more for greasing
4 large yellow onions, thinly sliced
1 teaspoon salt
¼ teaspoon black pepper
1 (8-ounce) baguette, cut into slices
1 teaspoon granulated sugar
8 cups beef broth

½ cup dry red wine
1 bay leaf
2 cups grated Gruyère

Directions

1. Melt the butter in a Dutch oven over medium heat. Add the onions, and season them with salt and pepper. Cover, and cook on medium-low heat for 45 minutes, stirring occasionally.
2. Meanwhile, preheat the oven to 350°F (177°C) and butter a baking sheet. Arrange the bread slices on the sheet and toast them in the oven until they are nicely browned, about 15 minutes. Turn them over halfway through. Set the toasted bread aside.
3. When the onions are cooked, raise the heat to medium-high and add the sugar. Cook until they are a deep golden brown.
4. Add the beef broth, wine, and bay leaf, and bring the pot to a boil. Lower the heat and simmer for about 10 minutes. Remove the bay leaf.
5. Preheat the broiler, and raise the oven rack to high.
6. Set out 6 heatproof bowls, and ladle soup into each. Top with a slice or two of bread, pressing it into the top of the liquid. Add a layer of cheese.
7. Broil until the cheese is melted and golden. Serve, and enjoy!

French Onion Dip

A favorite American dip that is typically made with cream cheese, milk, and dry onion soup mix. This dip will go great with crackers, cheese chips, and fresh vegetables as well. And it can be done in just a few minutes!

Serves 10 | Prep time 10 minutes

Ingredients
1 (8-ounce) package cream cheese, softened
¼ cup milk
1 (1-ounce) package dry onion soup mix

Directions

1. In a bowl, add all of the ingredients and mix until well combined.
2. Serve immediately.

Clam Dip

Dips were very popular in the 1960s and this family recipe was one of my favorite. This dip is prepared with clams, sour cream, or cream cheese and seasonings.

Serves 8 | Prep time 15 minutes

Ingredients
1 (8-ounce) can minced clams
8 ounces cream cheese, softened
3 garlic cloves, minced
¼ cup fresh parsley, chopped finely
2 teaspoons Worcestershire sauce
2 teaspoons fresh lemon juice
Dash of hot sauce
½ teaspoon Cajun seasoning

Ground black pepper, as required

Directions

1. Drain the can of clam, reserving about ¼ of the juice.
2. In a bowl, add all of the ingredients and mix until well combined.
3. Add the reserved clam juice and stir to combine.
4. Place the dip into a covered container and refrigerate for 2 hours or overnight before serving.

DESSERTS RECIPES

Mango Gelatin Salad

Either as an afternoon summer snack or dessert, this is one of my mom's favorite childhood recipes made by grandma. This dessert salad is prepared with mango, cream cheese, and gelatin.

Serves 8 | Prep time 15 minutes l Chill time 4 hours

Ingredients
Non-stick cooking spray
2 (15-ounce) cans diced mangoes, drained
1 (8-ounce) package cream cheese, softened and cubed
2 (3-ounce) packages lemon gelatin
1 (3-ounce) package apricot gelatin
2 cups boiling water
2 cups cold water

Directions

1. Grease a ring mold with cooking spray lightly. Set aside.
2. Add mangoes and cream cheese in a food processor and pulse until well combined.
3. In a large bowl, dissolve the gelatin in boiling water.
4. Add cold water and stir to combine.
5. Add mango mixture and stir until well combined.
6. Place the mixture into the prepared ring mold evenly and refrigerate for about 4 hours or until firm before serving.

Orange Mousse

A French recipe of dreamy and delicious mousse. This mousse will be a great addition to any dessert table. My Aunt Eunice's recipe is my definite favorite.

Serves 6 | Prep time 20 minutes | Cooking time 5 minutes

Ingredients
3 tablespoons orange liqueur
6-8 tablespoons orange zest, grated
½ teaspoon lemon zest, grated
1½-1¾ cups fresh orange juice
½ cup plus 1 tablespoon granulated sugar, divided
6 egg yolks
2 teaspoons cornstarch
6 egg whites
Pinch of salt
½ cup chilled whipping cream

Whipped cream, for topping

Directions

1. In a small bowl, mix the orange liqueur, orange, and lemon zest.
2. Add enough orange juice into the zest mixture so liquid measures 2 cups.
3. In another bowl, add ½ cup of the sugar and egg yolks and beat until pale yellow.
4. Add the cornstarch and juice mixture and beat until well combined.
5. Place the mixture into a saucepan over medium heat and cook for about 3-5 minutes or until slightly thickened, stirring continuously.
6. Remove from the heat and with a wire whisk, beat for about 30-40 seconds.
7. In a clean glass bowl, add the egg whites and salt and beat until soft peaks form.
8. Add the remaining sugar and beat until stiff peaks form.
9. Fold the egg whites into the hot orange mixture.
10. Place the bowl over the bowl of ice and gently stir until chilled completely.
11. In another small glass bowl, add the cream and beat until stiff.
12. Fold the whipped cream into the chilled mousse.
13. Transfer the mousse into serving bowls evenly.
14. Cover each bowl refrigerate overnight.
15. Serve with whipped cream if desired.

Baked Alaska

A classically delicious dessert during the 60s in America, this is a meringue dessert filled with ice cream that my grandmother always made for my grandfather's birthday.

Serves 16 | Prep time 20 minutes | Chill time 2 hours
Cooking time 35 minutes

Ingredients
8 cups vanilla ice cream, softened
Non-stick cooking spray
1 (18¼-ounce) package white cake mix
1 egg
½ teaspoon almond extract
1 cup white sugar

8 egg whites
⅛ teaspoon cream of tartar
⅛ teaspoon salt

Directions

1. Line the bottom and sides of an 8-inch round bowl with a piece of foil.
2. In the prepared bowl, place the ice cream and press firmly.
3. Cover the bowl and freeze for about 8 hours or until firm.
4. Preheat your oven to 350°F (177°C).
5. Grease and flour an 8x8 inch pan with cooking spray.
6. In a bowl, add the cake mix, egg, and almond extract and prepare according to the package's instructions.
7. Place the cake mixture into the prepared pan evenly.
8. Bake for about 20-25 minutes or according to the package's instructions.
9. Remove the cake pan from the oven and set aside to cool completely.
10. For meringue in a bowl, add the sugar, egg whites, cream of tartar, and salt and beat until stiff peaks form.
11. Line a baking sheet with parchment paper.
12. Remove the cake from the pan and place it onto the prepared baking sheet.
13. Invert the molded ice cream over the cake.
14. Immediately, spread the meringue over cake and ice cream evenly.
15. Freeze for about 2 hours.
16. Preheat oven to 425°F (218°C).
17. Arrange a rack in the lowest portion of the oven.
18. Bake for about 8-10 minutes, or until meringue is lightly browned.
19. Remove from the oven and serve immediately.

Burnt Custard

Found in magazines, throughout the 50s and 60s, my grandmother tried this dessert and soon perfected her own recipe that only has four ingredients.

Serves 6 | Prep time 15 minutes | Cooking time 45 minutes

Ingredients
½ cup plus 6 teaspoons sugar, divided
4 large egg yolks
2 cups heavy whipping cream
3 teaspoons vanilla extract

Directions

1.   Preheat the oven to 300°F (149°C).
2.   In a small bowl, add ½ cup of sugar and egg yolks and beat until well combined.
3.   In a small saucepan, add cream over medium heat and cook until

bubbles form.

4. Remove from the heat and slowly stir in some of the cream into the egg yolk mixture.
5. Return the cream mixture into the same pan, stirring continuously.
6. Add the vanilla extract and stir to combine.
7. Transfer the mixture to 6 (6-oz.) broiler-safe custard cups.
8. Arrange the custard cups into a baking dish.
9. Add about 1-inch of boiling water into the baking dish.
10. Bake, uncovered for about 30-35 minutes or until centers are just set.
11. Remove the ramekins from the oven and place them onto a wire rack to cool for about 10 minutes.
12. Cover each custard cup and refrigerate for at least 4 hours.
13. Remove from the refrigerator and set aside at room temperature for about 15 minutes before serving.
14. Now set the oven to broiler.
15. Arrange a rack about 8-ich from the heating element.
16. Sprinkle each custard cup with remaining sugar and broil for about 2-4 minutes or until sugar is caramelized.

Crème Caramel Custard

My personal vintage dessert favorite and another recipe passed down by my Mom. This delicious baked egg custard dessert will be great for the dessert table. This French-inspired baked caramel treat will be loved by all.

Serves 4 | Prep time 15 minutes | Cooking time 50 minutes
Chill time 12 hours

Ingredients
¾ cup sugar, divided
2 tablespoons water
1 vanilla bean, scraped out the seeds
2 cups whole milk
3 eggs
3 egg yolks

Directions

1. Preheat your oven to 300°F (149°C).
2. Arrange a rack in the lowest portion of the oven.
3. In a saucepan, add ½ cup of sugar and water over medium heat and cook until the sugar melts and a sauce forms, shaking the pan frequently.
4. Remove from the heat and place the caramel sauce into an ovenproof bowl evenly.
5. In another saucepan, add the milk, remaining sugar, and vanilla seeds over medium heat and cook just until the milk starts to smoke.
6. Remove from the heat and set aside.
7. In a bowl, beat the eggs until light and fluffy.
8. Slowly, add the eggs, a little at a time into the hot milk.\through a fine mesh strainer, strain the mixture into the bowl over the caramel sauce.
9. Arrange the bowl into a baking dish.
10. Add enough boiling water into the baking dish that covers the bottom third of the bowl.
11. Arrange the baking dish in the oven and immediately set the temperature to 350° F (177°c).
12. Bake for about 35-40 minutes.
13. Remove the bowl from the oven and place it onto a wire rack to cool completely.
14. Refrigerate overnight before serving.

Cherry Flan

This scrumptious dessert that's flavored with cherries is a family favorite and Aunt Eunice's recipe has been consistently present at family gatherings.

Serves 8 | Prep time 15 minutes | Cooking time 1 hour 2 minutes

Ingredients
1¼ cups milk
⅔ cup granulated sugar, divided
3 eggs
1 tablespoon vanilla extract
⅛ teaspoon salt
½ cup flour
3 cups black cherries, pitted

Directions

1. Preheat your oven to 350°F (149°C).

2.   Arrange a rack in the middle portion of the oven.
3.   In a blender, place milk, ⅓ cup sugar, the eggs, vanilla, salt, and flour, and pulse for about 1 minute.
4.   Place enough flour mixture into a baking dish and spread into a ¼-inch thick layer.
5.   Place the baking dish over medium heat for about 1-2 minutes.
6.   Remove from the heat and set aside.
7.   Spread the cherries over the batter and sprinkle with the remaining sugar.
8.   Place the remaining flour mixture on top and with the back of a spoon, smooth the top surface.
9.   Bake for about 1 hour.
10.   Remove from the oven and set aside for about 10 minutes before serving.

Jelly Roll

This was my absolute favorite when I was a little girl, and my kids love it too. It's the simplest recipe written by my Grandmother on a small bit of paper. It works every time.

Serves 6 | Prep. time 15 min. | Cooking time 15 min

Ingredients
<u>For the cake</u>
3 eggs
1 cup water
2 teaspoons baking powder
1 cup sugar
1 cup flour
1 teaspoon vanilla
Pinch salt
¾ cup jam of your choice

<u>For dusting</u>
¼ cup icing sugar

Directions

1. Preheat the oven to 350°F (177°C) and grease a 9x11-inch baking sheet.
2. Combine the ingredients and mix well. Spread them in the pan.
3. Bake 15 minutes, or until golden and cooked through.
4. Spread with jam and roll immediately. Dust with icing sugar.

Plum Crumb

A classic British-inspired dessert that became popular in the 60s, this is ideal when plums are in season.

Serves 8 | Prep time 15 minutes | Cooking time 45 minutes

Ingredients
Non-stick cooking spray
7 large plums, pitted and quartered
1 cup 3 plus tablespoons all-purpose flour, divided
½ cup packed brown sugar
1 teaspoon ground cinnamon
1 cup sugar
1 teaspoon baking powder
¼ teaspoon ground mace
¼ teaspoon salt
1 large egg, lightly beaten

½ cup butter, melted

Directions

1. Preheat your oven to 375°F (191°C).
2. Grease a 2-quart baking dish with cooking spray.
3. In a large bowl, add the plums, 3 tablespoons flour, brown sugar, and cinnamon, and mix well.
4. In a small bowl, add the remaining flour, sugar, baking powder, mace, and salt and mix well.
5. Add egg and with a fork, mix until crumbly.
6. Place the plum mixture into the prepared baking dish evenly and sprinkle it with sugar mixture.
7. Drizzle with the butter evenly.
8. Bake for about 40-45 minutes or until plums are tender and the top is golden brown.
9. Remove from the oven and set aside for about 10 minutes before serving.

Genoise Cake

This sponge cake is simple and made with eggs, sugar, flour, butter, and vanilla extract. It's one of the best cakes I've made, thanks to the no-fail recipe my mom made when I was growing up in the 1960s. She often added lemon flavoring.

Serves 12 | Prep time 15 minutes | Cooking time 35 minutes

Ingredients
2 tablespoons butter, softened
½ cup plus ⅓ cup plain bleached cake flour plus more for dusting
½ cup plus 1 tablespoon sugar, divided
¼ teaspoon salt
4 large eggs
1 teaspoon pure vanilla extract
¼ cup warm clarified butter
½ tablespoon orange liqueur (optional)

Directions

1. Preheat your oven to 350°F (177°C).
2. Grease a cake pan with most of the softened butter evenly.
3. Arrange a piece of wax paper in the bottom of the cake pan.
4. Then grease the wax paper with the remaining softened butter.
5. Arrange a rack onto the lower-middle position of the oven.
6. In a bowl, sift together the flour, 1 tablespoon of sugar, and salt.
7. In another bowl, add the remaining sugar, eggs, and vanilla extract and beat until well combined. You can add the orange liqueur during this step if using.
8. Add ¼ of the flour mixture and gently stir to combine.
9. Add the remaining flour mixture in 2 potions and stir to combine.
10. In a third large bowl, place the clarified butter.
11. Add some of the flour mixtures and gently stir to combine.
12. Fold the butter mixture into the remaining flour mixture.
13. Place the mixture into the prepared cake pan.
14. Lightly tap the pan on a counter to deflate bubbles.
15. Bake for about 30-35 minutes or until puffed and lightly browned.
16. Remove the cake pans from the oven and place them onto a wire rack for about 20 minutes.
17. Carefully invert each cake onto the wire rack to cool completely.

Lemon Chiffon Cake

An American cake that is unusually tender and moist. It's was a popular dessert in the 1960s, that is well worth revisiting. This cake is bursting with the refreshing touch of lemon.

Serves 16 | Prep time 15 minutes | Cooking time 55 minutes

Ingredients
Cake
2 cups cake flour
1½ cups sugar

1 tablespoon baking powder
½ teaspoon salt
½ cup low-fat sour cream
½ cup fat-free evaporated milk
¼ cup fresh lemon juice
2 tablespoons canola oil
2 teaspoons vanilla extract
1 teaspoon lemon extract
1 teaspoon lemon zest, grated
7 large egg whites
½ teaspoon cream of tartar

Lemon glaze
1¾ cups confectioners' sugar
3 tablespoons fresh lemon juice

Directions

1. Preheat the oven to 375ºF (191ºC). and place the oven rack in the middle position.
2. In a bowl, sift together the flour, sugar, baking powder, and salt.
3. In another large bowl, add the sour cream, evaporated milk, lemon juice, oil, vanilla extract, lemon extract, and lemon zest and beat until well combined.
4. Slowly, add the flour mixture and mix until smooth.
5. In a small glass bowl, add the egg whites and beat until foamy.
6. Add cream of tartar and beat until stiff peaks form.
7. Gently fold the whipped egg whites into the lemon mixture.
8. Place the mixture into an ungreased 10-inch tube pan.
9. Bake for about 40-55 minutes or until cake springs back when lightly touched.
10. Remove from the oven and immediately invert the cake onto a wire rack to cool completely.
11. Meanwhile, for the glaze: in a bowl, add the sugar and lemon juice and beat until well combined.
12. Drizzle the glaze over the cake and serve.

Chocolate Cake

This cake has been a dream for chocolate lovers since the 60s and mine as well. My Aunt Eunice's recipes never fail me, including this cake.

Serves 16 | Prep time 20 minutes | Cooking time 37 minutes

Ingredients
Cake
Non-stick cooking spray
2⅔ cups all-purpose flour plus more for dusting
¾ cup baking cocoa
3 teaspoons baking soda
½ teaspoon salt
3 cups packed brown sugar
1 cup butter, softened
4 large eggs
2 teaspoons vanilla extract

1 ⅓ cups sour cream
1 ⅓ cups boiling water

Frosting
3 ounces semisweet chocolate, chopped
3 ounces unsweetened chocolate, chopped
½ cup butter, cubed
5 cups confectioners' sugar
1 cup sour cream
2 teaspoons vanilla extract

Directions

1. Preheat your oven to 350°F (177°C).
2. Grease 3 (9-inch) round cake pans with cooking spray and then dust each with a little flour.
3. For the cake: in a large bowl, mix together the flour, cocoa, baking soda, and salt.
4. In another large bowl, add brown sugar and butter and beat until light and fluffy.
5. Add eggs, 1 at a time, beating well after each addition.
6. Add vanilla extract and beat until well combined.
7. Add the flour mixture alternately with sour cream, beating well after each addition.
8. Add water and mix until well combined.
9. Divide the mixture into the prepared cake pans evenly.
10. Bake for about 30-35 minutes or until a wooden skewer inserted in the center comes out clean,
11. Remove the cake pans from the oven and place them onto a wire rack for about 10 minutes.
12. Carefully invert each cake onto the wire rack to cool completely.
13. For the frosting: in a microwave-safe bowl, add chocolates and butter and microwave on high for about 1½-2 minutes or until melted completely, stirring after every 30 seconds.
14. Remove from microwave and stir until smooth.
15. Set aside to cool slightly.
16. In a large bowl, add confectioners' sugar, sour cream, and vanilla extract and beat until well combined.

17. Add chocolate mixture and beat until smooth.
18. Spread frosting between the layers and over top and sides of the cake and serve.

APPENDIX

Cooking Conversion Charts

1. Measuring Equivalent Chart

Type	Imperial	Imperial	Metric
Weight	1 dry ounce		28g
	1 pound	16 dry ounces	0.45 kg
Volume	1 teaspoon		5 ml
	1 dessert spoon	2 teaspoons	10 ml
	1 tablespoon	3 teaspoons	15 ml
	1 Australian tablespoon	4 teaspoons	20 ml
	1 fluid ounce	2 tablespoons	30 ml
	1 cup	16 tablespoons	240 ml
	1 cup	8 fluid ounces	240 ml
	1 pint	2 cups	470 ml
	1 quart	2 pints	0.95 l
	1 gallon	4 quarts	3.8 l
Length	1 inch		2.54 cm

Numbers are rounded to the closest equivalent

2. Oven Temperature Equivalent Chart

Fahrenheit (°F)	Celsius (°C)	Gas Mark
220	100	
225	110	1/4
250	120	½
275	140	1
300	150	2
325	160	3
350	180	4
375	190	5
400	200	6
425	220	7
450	230	8
475	250	9
500	260	

* Celsius (°C) = T (°F)-32] * 5/9

** Fahrenheit (°F) = T (°C) * 9/5 + 32

*** Numbers are rounded to the closest equivalent